I0437435

OBAMA'S PEACE IN THE MIDDLE EAST

The Mideast Peace Process

Ali Abdul Rashid

authorHOUSE®

AuthorHouse™
1663 Liberty Drive, Suite 200
Bloomington, IN 47403
www.authorhouse.com
Phone: 1-800-839-8640

© 2009 Ali Abdul Rashid. All rights reserved.

No part of this book may be reproduced, stored in
a retrieval system, or transmitted by any means
without the written permission of the author.

First published by AuthorHouse 5/22/2009

ISBN: 978-1-4389-7106-3 (sc)

Printed in the United States of America
Bloomington, Indiana

This book is printed on acid-free paper.

TABLE OF CONTENTS

Obama's Peace in the Middle East

The Mideast Peace Process

Change has come to America with the historic election of Barack Hussein Obama, the first African-American president of the United States. President Obama has captured the vision of America, and his rise to the White House transcends the color line of racism, oppression, and segregation, and sends hope to the world for peace. Although the racist mindset of white supremacy is still prevalent, the will of the people has spoken; the fundamental principles of democracy and free will and free speech have elected a new commander-in-chief of our great nation. In spite of the many attempts of past administrations, and the most recent, the Bush administration to broker peace between two historic adversaries, the Israelis and the Palestinians, no one is more qualified than President Obama to make peace in the Middle East. His mentality is devoid of the racism and favoritism that has dominated the minds of previous administrations, and he is a man of integrity. He is extremely intelligent, and he has assembled a team of advisors called "The Dream Team," who share his vision of uniting America. President Obama is on a universal mission to bring unity to a divided nation, establish peace in the Middle East, and promote world peace. He is the embodiment of the people's will, and it is with that spirit that unity and brother-/sisterhood will be achieved on the domestic front, as well as abroad. The world is in search of peace, racial acceptance, and religious tolerance, and with the unprecedented turnout on November 4, 2008 for the presidential election, the movement has begun.

America is undoubtedly a great nation, but it would be a greater nation if we worked to eliminate the racist mentality of white supremacy that has divided us for too long. The idea that one race is innately more intellectually superior than the other must not be given a platform in any forum. With the historical turnout on November 4, 2008, it seems that our nation is moving in the right direction to bridge the racial divide. The window of opportunity is open to change the course of our nation, and we must not allow it to close before we are united as one. We must support the vision of America that President Obama has skillfully articulated, and we must remove from our minds any doubt that he is a visionary who will lead this country in the right direction. Change is on the horizon, but substantial change does not happen overnight. It is a gradual process that requires patience, diligence, and persistence. Just as the citizens of this nation came out to exercise their right to vote, we must encourage the exercise of freedoms that demonstrate the strength of our democracy. We must continue to seek ways to improve the quality of life for all people, in spite of their religious beliefs, sexual orientation, or political views. During the election, there were an overwhelming number of African Americans and Hispanics who supported and voted for President Obama; however, there were still many who were not captured by his vision. Similarly, a large number of whites, Asians, and Native Americans supported and voted for him, while a substantial number did not. Ironically, the Jewish community was ambivalent. Many Jewish people did not support or vote for him for several reasons. Their reluctance was not the result of racism or his lack of experience. Rather, it was his name, his relationship with his pastor, and his religion that were in question. It had been said that he was a Muslim, and many thought that he would be biased toward Islam because his father was a Muslim, although he is a Christian and his roots are connected to the soil of Kenya. In light of those situations, many Jewish people falsely believed that he would be more sympathetic toward the Palestinian cause. That assumption was predicated upon factual information regarding his heritage, but it has no relevance on his performance as president of the United States of America. Another reason for their lack of support was because he had mentioned on several occasions during his campaign that he would have a dialogue with President Mahmoud Ahmadinejad of Iran, without preconditions. President Ahmadinejad is a charismatic and influential leader who denies the Holocaust ever happened, and has vowed to wipe Israel off the map. However, as sensitive as it may be, President Obama understands that the complicated road to peace in the Middle East has historically been difficult, and further isolation and arrogance will only widen the divide. President Obama must be given the opportunity to pursue and broker peace as he and his administration advise. Now that he has selected Rahm Emanuel as chief of staff, the Jewish community has changed their perception of him. The state of

Israel and the American Jewish community are more relaxed because Mr. Emanuel is Jewish, with roots in Israel. Additionally, now that the former first lady, Hillary Rodham Clinton, has been confirmed as the secretary of state, the state of Israel remains confident that America will continue to be its strongest Western supporter. Secretary Clinton has made several trips to Israel during the eight years she served as first lady, and she also visited the Jewish state during her presidential campaign. At this point, peace in the Middle East can only be established through open dialogue with sincere visionaries seeking to change the course of history. History has proven that peace can never be sustained through violence. In contrast, Mr. Emanuel's selection as chief of staff has generated condemnation from Ayman al-Zawahiri, one of the leaders of al Qaeda. He has attempted to discredit President Obama's integrity and his leadership ability. He has stated that he has abandoned his roots, and has advanced to the highest office in the land because he supports the "criminals in America," and supports the Jewish state of Israel. He further stated that President Obama is just a token only to be used as a pawn for the Zionist nation. Ayman al-Zawahiri has repeated his threats to bring destruction to America, and encourages all Muslims to "fight the infidels of America." Al-Zawahiri's call for jihad against the United States is a call that will fall on the ears of a small sector of Muslims who share his misguided concepts of Islam. The religion of Islam is a religion of peace. It does not advocate violence, particularly the killing of innocent men, women, and children. It respects all religions instituted by the Creator, and advocates mutual consultation to resolve disagreements and disputes. Unfortunately, Islam has been cast in a dim light by Muslims who do not represent or practice the religion as it was instituted and practiced universally. However, President Obama is astute, and well versed in both religion and politics. America is indeed a democratic nation governed by a living constitution that represents the will of all Americans. America recognizes the right of free speech, free elections, and respect for individual religious freedom, as President Obama so elegantly expressed during his inaugural speech. These are examples of freedoms that make America a great nation, and in order for our country to continue to enjoy these freedoms and prosper, al Qaeda must be "stamped out." Our government must be proactive and utilize all resources to prevent the leaders of al Qaeda from executing another terrorist attack on our soil.

The political climate in the Middle East has always been unpredictable; however, after many setbacks and delays in holding elections in the Palestinian territories, elections were finally held in Gaza and the West Bank in January 2006, and the radical group Hamas won. The Palestinians overwhelmingly voted, giving Hamas a landslide victory over Fatah. Along with the unpopular win came 76 of 132 seats in parliament versus 43 for Fatah. Nevertheless, the Palestine Liberation Organization (or Fatah) was recognized as the legitimate government, and both Israel and America recognized it as such. Fatah had renounced violence and was seeking peace with Israel. Conversely, the legitimacy of Hamas was not recognized because it is regarded as a terrorist organization by both Israel and the United States. Therefore, their leaders were rejected and consequently targeted for assassination. As a result of Hamas's refusal to recognize Israel and renounce violence, Israel cut off financial aid, and the United States immediately instituted sanctions. Shortly thereafter, fighting to establish control of the area broke out between the two rival organizations (Hamas and Fatah) and bodies began to fall on both sides. Hamas forcibly won control of the Gaza Strip, leaving Fatah in control of the West Bank. Meanwhile, Hamas vowed to continue its arms resistance against Israel to recover land that was lost during the Six Day War in 1967, while Israel refuses to recognize Hamas as a legitimate government, and continues to target its leaders for air strikes. At any rate, peace can only be achieved in the Middle East when both Israel and the United States reach the point of awakening that Hamas must be recognized as the legitimate representative of the Palestinian people. Currently, President Mahmood Abbas is recognized as president of the Palestinians, although the democratic election proves otherwise. Recognition of Hamas does not and will not promote, condone, or legitimize terrorism. Rather, it acknowledges the will of the people to elect their own leaders and government, and move the region one step closer to peace. As part of any peace agreement, the state of Israel must abandon the hundreds of settlements built on Palestinian land in the West Bank. It is estimated that hundreds of settlements have been built, and that more than 60,000 settlers have settled there after Israel captured the land during the Six Day War. The Israeli government must devise a plan to relocate the settlers and surrender the land without destroying the settlements. Maintaining the settlements may appear to be insignificant in light of all the other complicated and serious issues to be negotiated, but it would be a goodwill gesture toward establishing peace. Also, it would defer the cost of reconstruction, as well as provide immediate homes for the thousands of Palestinians who have been displaced by years of war and who are now living in refugee camps throughout the various territories. Unlike the arrogant and naive George W. Bush, Barack H. Obama is the president who can bring peace to the Middle East. He is honest, he is passionate, and he has integrity. But more importantly, he is not biased toward Hamas, Fatah, or Israel. He understands the struggles of both the Palestinians and the Israelis, and he is cognizant of the significance of sacred land beholden to both. George W. Bush failed to understand the culture and mindset of Muslims, particularly the Palestinians. This was evident in his 2004 State of the Union address, in which he stated to the late Chairman Yasser Arafat, who was confined to his headquarters in the compound of Ramallah by the Israelis who had surrounded the compound with tanks: **"Chairman Arafat, I want you to tell your people to stop blowing themselves up in an attempt to resolve issues that can be handled diplomatically. I don't understand it; suicide is crazy."** That statement was made in response to the suicide bombers who had penetrated the Israeli defenses and detonated body explosives in the marketplace, which wounded and killed numerous innocent civilians. If former president Bush had understood the culture and mindset of Muslims fighting against oppression and militarily domination, he would have understood the concept of martyrdom, fighting, and dying in the way of *fas-salbillah,* in the way of Allah. Martyrdom is a fundamental belief in Islam; all Muslims should have some type of understanding of its concept, and would love to experience if spiritually chosen for the ultimate sacrifice. It is not only the act of wearing a vest filled with explosives with a target enemy in mind; it is also the act of preventing or removing an oppressive situation or condition wherever it may exist, and it is certainly not an act of suicide as defined by secular thought. Muslims who desire to become terrorists must develop a certain mindset that is remarkably different from the average Muslim, in spite of the *madhhab* (school of thought) they follow. They usually devote themselves to a particular cause, religious or otherwise, and justify their actions based on their understanding and interpretation of the Holy Qu'ran. In most cases, Muslims who resort to the act of terrorism have stepped outside the rim of *figh* (Islamic Law), but they justify their actions in the name of the religion. In a similar regard, a Muslim who seeks to make the ultimate sacrifice—and become a suicide bomber, for example— must be strong in his or her faith, not crazy. The motivation must be to preserve and/or defend the religion, believing the reward to be paradise. On the other hand, seeking the ultimate sacrifice for any other reason may be justified in the mind of the individual or organization that perpetuates the act, but it is neither justified nor supported by the teachings of Islam. For instance, an individual should not be motivated to commit the act because of a debilitating or terminal illness. Likewise, being commissioned to carry out the act for family monetary gain is also beyond the scope of the religion. In essence, it is the intent preceding the act that determines the ultimate reward or punishment. In Islamic countries, preparing one to become a suicide bomber is not always a difficult task, depending on the motive, the influence, and their understanding of the religion. Understanding that reality in its proper contexts would have allowed Bush to be more effective in establishing a dialogue with the Palestinian authorities. Rather, he highlighted his ignorance by referring to the act as being "crazy" during his State of the Union address, and it showed his views regarding Islam were narrow and misinformed. The aforementioned statement by President Bush sent a clear message to the Arab world that he was not in tune with the reality of Islamic society. In contrast, President Obama is smarter and more insightful. He is spiritually in tune with not only the American people, but he is also spiritually and emotionally connected to the good-willed people in the international community, which includes the Arab world. His efforts to achieve peace in the Middle East will be supported by the will of the people, because he is on a divine mission, and the work he is commissioned to do is beyond the reach of man's interference. Indeed, we are at the international crossroads of history, and President Obama understands the true meaning of extending the olive branch of peace. The time for change has indeed come to America, and peace can be established in the Middle East, God willing. With the exception of the terrorist organizations and the extremists who will kill and die to hinder peace, the perception of the world has changed toward America with the election of the first African-American president. In spite of the fact that the more radical organizations—al Qaeda, Hamas, Islamic Jihad, and Hezbollah—still refuse to entertain peace with Israel, peace accords are being discussed with Arab states such as Egypt, Jordan, and Syria. In 2001, the attack on New York's Twin Towers, the Pentagon, and the failed attempt at the White House with the jetliner going down in the hills of Pennsylvania were horrific acts designed to protest America's foreign policy as it related to its strong support for Israel. From the mindset of the terrorists, any opposition toward America is opposition toward Israel and vice versa. Notwithstanding the above, the martyrdom mission was also an act to embarrass the Bush administration. The simultaneous aerial attacks also showed just how vulnerable our nation's defenses were, and it left the American people in a state of shock. The attacks embedded psychological fear in the minds of most Americans, and the threat of another attack still lingers, especially when videos are broadcast on national and world news of an infamous terrorist condemning America. Quite frankly, as long as there are American soldiers defending foreign land in countries such as Afghanistan and Iraq, the possibility of further attacks is real. Unfortunately, there have been too many examples of inconceivable acts of violence, and too many innocent lives have been lost, to not take all threats seriously. Our nation must not live in fear, and we must be prepared and ready to defend our freedoms at all costs. Recently, The Israeli government released more than 200 prisoners in December 2008, as a goodwill gesture toward establishing peace. Several weeks later, the six-month truce between Israel and Hamas ended, and blood began to flow in the streets of Gaza. The Israeli Defense Force launched air strikes for three weeks on specific sites, killing more than 1,300 people (including a countless numbers of civilians) and more than 5,000 were wounded. The leaders of Hamas called the attack a massacre and vowed to continue fighting for their land. When the facts of this conflict are examine very objectively, it is clear that Hamas has repeatedly fired rockets at Israel, but their attacks have killed about thirteen innocent people, and property damage has been minimal. Conversely, Israeli air strikes have killed more than 1,300 people (of which 410 were children) during the course of 22 days. Hamas's supreme leader, Khaled Meshal, has called for a new *intifada* (or uprising) against Israel; the streets of Gaza, the West Bank, and Israel will be renewed with blood. The governments of Egypt, Jordan, Syria, and Saudi Arabia have made several attempts in the past to broker peace between the Palestinians and Israel, but Hamas refuses to recognize Israel's right to exist, and Israel refuses to recognize Hamas as the legitimate government for its people. Although there have been agreements of a cease fire, the aftermath has left catastrophic damage to an untold number of innocent men, women, and children. Prior to the ceasefire, the United Nations' secretary general, Ban Ki-moon, accused the Israeli authorities of using white phosphorous shells during the conflict, which is considered by many to be against the Geneva Conventions Rules of International Law when they are used on civilian population. Phosphorous shells are a compound that can cause severe eye irritation. It burns the skin to the bone, and it can also cause respiratory problems if not treated immediately. However, the

Israeli government ignored Secretary General Ban Ki-moon's pleas to stop the killing. Now that the rockets have stop firing and the tanks are silent, a permanent cease fire will only happen when there are direct talks between Hamas leadership and Israeli leaders. The idea of not talking with leaders of a terrorist organization appears to be the barrier that prevents a permanent resolution to the conflict and justifies future attacks by the Israeli government. Hamas leaders must be brought into the equation before either state can have peace. As it is pursued by all parties, long-term peace is the goal, and it can only be achieved when there is a trilateral agreement between the Israeli government, Fatah, and Hamas. President Abbas has proven to be a strong and insightful leader, and the dream of statehood for his people can become a reality when certain conditions are met. The major condition, however, is beyond his control. He cannot convince Hamas's leadership to renounce violence and recognize Israel's right to exist in peace in spite of his best efforts. Therefore, the land mines on the road to peace will continue to explode, and any past accomplishments will be lost. America's light has just begun to shine in the Middle East with the election of President Obama, and the climate is right for U.S. intervention. Our government must act now to aggressively design a peace accord that will satisfy the demands of these governments before another outbreak of war occurs. The framework has already been drafted in the road map to peace by Egypt, Saudi Arabia, Israel, and the Bush administration, and the conditions can be met. Particularly, now that President Obama has selected Hillary Rodham Clinton as secretary of state, and with the appointment of George Mitchell as the Mideast envoy, substantial progress can be made in the region. However, the Israeli government has been adamant about refusing to negotiate with Hamas because it has been branded a terrorist organization. Nevertheless, the mortar attacks—and for the most part, the suicide bombers—have been commissioned by the Hamas organization, not Fatah. Therefore, it would make good moral sense to open a dialogue with Hamas's leadership, and the talks must take place without preconditions. Establishing statehood, opening the borders to Egypt and Jordan, and the right of return for the Palestinians living in exile must be the main focal points of any discussion. At this point, it appears the Israeli government is sincere about wanting peace in the region, but as long as it continues to sidestep the issue of direct negotiations, peace will only be short lived at best. Of course, renouncing violence and recognizing Israel's right to exist should be the main focal points of discussion for Israel, just as Hamas has their focal points. That level of dialogue must take place before the recurrence of another war, which will undoubtedly involve militants from the surrounding region and will transform the course of the war. However, when high-level talks are held and statehood is given to the Palestinians, the governments of Fatah and Hamas will be united and the citizens of Israel will live in peace. When that dream becomes a reality, only then will the Iranian promises of the annihilation of Israel no longer be a threat. In spite of any difference (whether real or perceived) on behalf of the respective governments, the Iranian government—as well as those of Egypt, Jordan, Turkey, and Saudi Arabia—will have a moral and religious obligation to support the Palestinian people, just as the United States supports Israel unconditionally. When the above have been achieved, the influence of a unified government will be the embodiment of the people's will for peace. However, during the recent conflict, it seemed that the Israeli government was trying to annihilate the Palestinians without making an official declaration by conducting excessive military operations against Hamas. Although the war targeted specific sites in Gaza—Hamas's stronghold—hundreds have died, several hundreds more have been injured, and far more have being displaced. The city infrastructure was completely destroyed, and life in the refugee camps has been a living hell. There is still limited food, water, and medical supplies, and the rubble of bricks seems to be their only means of shelter. Just as the world witnessed and remained silent when the 6 million innocent men, women, and Jewish children died during the Holocaust, the world witnessed the massacre of the Palestinian people, and remained relatively silent. Although there was mass protest around the world condemning the attacks, no country took steps to directly intervene to demand cease fire. As a result of these atrocities committed by the Israeli government, a new wave of terror is imminent for our nation. The Mideast perception is that the Bush administration not only condoned the attacks but encouraged them by placing the blame squarely on the Hamas organization. Undoubtedly, Hamas should be strongly condemned for its rocket attacks against Israel, but the international community, and particularly the Arab states, should feel a sense of shame for remaining so quiet and being so inactive during the massacre. The Palestinian people are still in a humanitarian crisis, and only a few organizations have responded with aid. The heroic efforts of the Red Cross and the United Nations workers should be commended for delivering aid under fire when their safety was never guaranteed. The American government should have taken a lead role in resolving this crisis. Instead, Washington remained silent while the population perished. Nevertheless, now that President Obama is the commander in chief, at some point, he must make a public statement repudiating the attacks. He must take a firm stand against both Israel and Hamas to regain America's lost credibility, and position himself to broker peace. Israel had a right to defend itself and protect its citizens, but the massive and excessive force that was used to prevent rocket attacks appears to be criminal and unjustified. The Israeli Defense Force has used Apache helicopters, warships, and F-15 fighter jets provided by the U.S. government to obliterate Hamas and the Palestinian people. The IDF was on a search-and-destroy mission to not only destroy the infrastructure of the terrorist network, but also to kill as many Palestinians as possible. The ground invasion of Gaza was designed to systematically go from house to house and kill anyone who had the potential to threaten Israel. The leaders of the Israeli government should be indicted for committing crimes against humanity, and the world court should hold them accountable for their actions. If any other government had committed these horrific acts of human destruction, the United States would have been the first nation to express condemnation, as we have done in the past. Instead, it seems to be a double standard, because the Bush administration blamed Hamas for initiating the war by ending the six-month truce. Consequently, no suggestion of a cease fire was mentioned until at least 1,000 were dead. The Israeli government stated their military operation would continue until its goal of incapacitating Hamas was met. Given the massive force that was being used, their goal was met in twenty-two days. However, even a death toll of more than a thousand will not stop the arms struggle. Too many people have died. Too many lives have been destroyed, and too much blood has stained the streets of Gaza to abandon the jihad. The supreme leader of Hamas, Khaled Meshal, living in exile in Syria, has called for a new *intifada* against Israel. The mindset of the suicide bomber, while praying for peace, is still preparing for martyrdom. The Middle East is still in a humanitarian crisis, and if a peace accord is not accepted by Israel and the Palestinians, the dream of statehood and peace for Israel will remain just a dream for the people in that region. During the conflict, it was quite a contradiction on behalf of the Israeli government to briefly suspend their massive attacks to permit the Red Cross and U.N. workers to provide humanitarian aid, only to resume the massacre of the Palestinian people when the smoke cleared.

President Abbas has met with Israeli leaders on a number of occasions to try to find a permanent solution to the ongoing crisis. Although his intentions may have been good, he lost the confidence of his people and can no longer be an effective leader. He has been called a traitor and an Israeli collaborator, and his organization has been accused of spying for Israel to facilitate assassinations of Hamas's leaders. These accusations are so strong that they effectively render him incapable of representing and negotiating on behalf of the Palestinian people. In spite of the direct contacts, little progress has been made during his meetings with American and Israeli officials. Time is definitely not on his side as the end of his presidential term rapidly approaches, and life in Gaza and the West Bank remains uncertain for his people. For the past sixty years, there have been different levels of conflict in the region between the Arab nation and Israel. However, this most recent conflict has highlighted to the world the true nature and intentions of the Israeli government. They have literally destroyed the homes, schools, hospitals, and mosques of the Palestinian people, and so many civilians have been killed that peace will be extremely difficult to reach. Our government must make this issue a top priority. Our new secretary of state, Hillary Rodham Clinton, along with the Mideast envoy, George

Mitchell, must be the trailblazers who will allow President Obama to get the leaders of that region to accept a permanent commitment of peace. As the result of promoting peace in the Middle East, and for following the vision of his predecessor, Anwar al Sadat, who was a courageous leader who accepted peace with Israel, President Muhammad Hosni Mubarak of Egypt has been a target for assassination ever since he became president. Anwar al Sadat was the first leader of an Arab state to enter into peace with Israel, in 1978 during the Camp David Accords, following its defeat of the Six Day War in 1967. Consequently, on October 6, 1981, he was assassinated by high-ranking members of his military. Similarly, Yitzhak Rabin, the prime minister of Israel—who was pursuing peace with the Palestinians under the leadership of the late chairman, Yasser Arafat, during the Oslo Peace Process—was assassinated in Tel Aviv on November 4, 1995, by a young Jewish extremist. The cycle of violence in the Middle East seems to always re-occur when the possibility of peace appears to be within reach. However, historically, peace in the region has always been fragile and short-lived at best, and the visionaries who desired peace for their people after years of conflict paid the ultimate price. Their lives were taken in the pursuit of peace, but they died with dignity and respect. Here we are at the crossroads of history, and we are fighting an extension of the same war, but under different circumstances. The strategies may have changed, and there is a new generation of fighters, but the core issues remain and peace is still elusive. Currently, the road to peace in the Middle East is similar to that of a road filled with active land mines. One wrong move can be a fatal mistake, causing many to lose their lives. Therefore, all steps must be taken very cautiously, and the inroads to peace must be properly navigated and negotiated by men and women who have captured the vision.

The Absence of Weapons of Mass Destruction

It is the belief of many Americans that the Bush administration intentionally misled the Congress and the American people by saying the late Saddam Hussein had weapons of mass destruction, and in order to keep America safe, it was our moral responsibility to destroy the stockpile of chemical and deadly explosives. Therefore, an executive order was issued and in March 2003, we proceeded to invade Iraq along with British troops. The allied forces invaded by land, air, and sea, and we toppled the government while killing thousands of Iraqi soldiers who stood up to defend their country. After the bombs fell and the smoke cleared, our inspectors began to search for the WMD in the various locations our intelligence information said they were stored. The search continued for weeks, weeks turned into months, and surprisingly, no WMD were found. Saddam Hussein ran to avoid being captured, while his two sons, Odai and Qusai were killed, and their pictures broadcast around the world. Months passed while the search for Saddam Hussein continued, and many of his close advisers were either captured or killed. Then on December 13, 2003, the American soldiers captured the lone fugitive. He was found hiding in a dark hole about eight feet deep near the city of Tikrit. Once discovered, he offered no resistance and his days before the gallows were numbered. Saddam Hussein was tried in his own country according to the Sharia, the jurisprudence of Islam, and convicted by his own peers. He was convicted on November 5, 2006 of various crimes against humanity, and sentenced to death by hanging. Saddam Hussein was hanged in the city of Baghdad on December 30, 2006. It has also been the belief of many politically informed individuals (without any factual information to support their theory) that the invasion of Iraq was really a pretext to get closer to Iran to position our military for combat. It is believed the initial plan was to threaten President Admadinejad to abandon the production of nuclear energy or face the possibility of an attack. The objective was to bomb specific sites that our intelligence had confirmed were nuclear manufacturing plants. However, the anticipated conquest of Iraq was not accomplished as soon as was projected due the outbreak of civil war within the region, and the deadly attacks on American soldiers. The Sunni began fighting the Shiites, and both began attacking the Kurds. This left the American soldiers caught in the middle of a conflict, trying to stabilize a region while being under attack from militants from all sides. Consequently, the plan to attack Iran's manufacturing sites and move further east into Iran was reconsidered. Our government had already deployed more than 120,000 soldiers to Iraq, more than 30,000 to Afghanistan, and the American people had begun protesting the war. Our military was already engaged in combat on two fronts, and our Congress had begun hearings to determine the status of the war and whether a new strategy should be considered. Now that the republic of Iran is believed to have the capability to manufacture a nuclear bomb, and with George W. Bush's presidential term rapidly coming to an end, the decision to make a pre-emptive strike was wisely taken off the table. However, the state of Israel is still cognizant of the threatening remarks made by President Admadinejad, and the decision to attack its nuclear sites has not been ruled out. It is also believed that former president Bush had a private conversation with Israeli president

Shimon Peres regarding an attack on Iran, and he wisely discouraged a pre-emptive attack. It is believed that he thought attacking Iran and destroying its nuclear sites was the right thing to do, but it would undoubtedly initiate a war that our military was not prepared to get involved with, even though Israel is our strongest ally in the Middle East. The rationale is that the Arab states (Turkey, Jordan, Syria, and Lebanon) would unite and commence a concerted attack to eliminate the Jewish state. In any event, President Admadinejad has stated Iran has a right to produce nuclear energy for peaceful purposes, and he has no plan of abandoning its mission. Whether his position is right or wrong, at this point, the only way to reach a reasonable solution is through diplomatic means, because the threat of force by the United States, Israel, and perhaps Britain would only exacerbate the situation and create further isolation. A military confrontation with Iran at this point would compromise our nation's security, divide our nation even further, and discredit Obama's credibility around the world. The citizens of the Middle East would become more hostile toward Americans living abroad, whose lives would be in danger because an attack against Iran would essentially be an attack on Islam. Such an attack would reinforce the belief of Muslims throughout the world that America's goal is to extinguish the light of

Islam, further promoting anti-American sentiments often expressed by hate and terrorist organizations. Additionally, the influence of the terrorist ideology will become more prevalent abroad, negating all hope for peace in the Middle East. Also, the manifestation of homegrown terrorism would become more evident from foreign Muslims born and living in the United States, as well as from American-born Muslims who are disgruntled with the government and who believe that Muslims are generally discriminated against because of their religion. Our government must learn from our past mistakes, especially in Afghanistan, and a war with Iran would be equivalent to pulling the pin that could possibly trigger the bomb. Our government must be smarter; our goal should be to pursue peace rather than declare war, perhaps even a nuclear war.

Since the invasion of Afghanistan by the U.S.-led coalition in 2001, approximately 1,100 American soldiers have fallen versus more than 100,000 Muslims, and the body count increases daily on both sides of the barrel. The perception of many Muslims in the Arab world is that military engagements such as this are exactly what were previously mentioned: an attempt by the United States government to extinguish the light of Islam in the Middle East. The perception here is similar to that of the statement made by Mahmoud

Ahmadinejad, the president of Iran, to wipe Israel of the map. Without America making a similar declaration, the action is the same. Afghanistan has been the battleground that has caused the deaths of thousands of militant soldiers—and thousands of innocent civilian women and children. Now that there has been a degree of stability in the region with the overwhelming presence of U.S. and coalition forces, President Hamib Karzai realize that it can only be sustained by continuous dialogue with Mullah Mohammed Omar, the leader of the Taliban. In that regard, he has encouraged the Taliban militants to cease the violence and participate in the government. Unlike the coalition force commander, President Karzai understands that peace can never be achieved in the region without Taliban representation in the government. He also understands that he will always be a target for assassination if peace is not reached between the two forces, primarily because his rise to power came as the result of U.S. intervention, and the fact that he welcomed the coalition forces. A lesson from the pages of history can be learned from the 1953 coup in Iran that installed Shah Mohammad Reza Pahlavi. Even though the shah maintained power for decades with the support of Washington, he was always a target for assassination until his exile in 1979 when the Islamic Revolution took control of the country. Similarly, President Karzai's fate lies in the will of the Afghan people, and if he continues to advocate support for the continued presence of coalition forces, that will negate any possibility of having Taliban representation in the government; consequently, he will suffer the same fate as the shah or he will fall to an assassin's bullet, as the late Benazir Bhutto of Pakistan did. Afghanistan is struggling to become a sovereign nation, and that cannot happen with the continuous presence of American soldiers occupying the land. At this point, the Pentagon has not made a definitive decision to withdraw soldiers from Afghanistan. In fact, President Obama has stated his intentions are to decrease the number of troops in Iraq and increase the numbers in Afghanistan. In that regard, a decision to withdraw troops from Iraq has been mapped out leaving one to speculate about Afghanistan. As reported by CNN, the plan is to have a substantial withdrawal of American soldiers by June 30, 2009, and a complete withdrawal by December 31, 2011. That is definitely a step in the right direction, and the Iraqi people are waiting to celebrate. The proposed timetable for the withdrawal is very appropriate and it will not compromise our national security. However, to reiterate a fact, peace and stability in Afghanistan can only be achieved with the Taliban support. Otherwise, fighting will continue, and the Afghan government, as well as its army, will be targeted just as the American soldiers are being targeted. The insurgents will continue their attacks until either all the Muslims are killed or all the foreign soldiers are withdrawn from the land. At this point, the Iranian government has not deployed any soldiers to either Afghanistan or Iraq, but that is subject to change. Nevertheless, our intelligence sources have stated that Iran has provided logistical support such as funding, intelligence, and weapons—accusations the Iranian government has strongly denied. If the war in Afghanistan does not end within the first two years of the Obama's administration, it is reasonable to believe that our military will be fully engaged in combat with Iran by December 31, 2011, the date for the complete withdrawal of American troops from Iraq. If that does happen for whatever reason, that would lead our country down the road to disaster. That will bring us one step closer to the possibility of a nuclear confrontation, not only with Iran, but possibly with Pakistan as well. As it has been reported by many news sources, the war in Afghanistan has escalated; the U.S. allied forces are not only fighting against the resistance of the Taliban and al Qaeda, but militants from Pakistan are also launching deadly attacks. Convoys carrying food, fuel, and medical equipment to the coalition forces are being destroyed near the Pakistan-Afghanistan border, and the death toll is rising. The intense fighting will continue much longer than Washington ever imagined, because the militants are on a holy mission and they refuse to lay down their arms. At this point, the only way the war can be de-escalated and perhaps come to an end is if Mullah Omar accepts the peace offer extended by President Karzai. That would be a strategic move that would stop the attacks on U.S. and NATO soldiers, and it would allow our government to draft a realistic plan for the withdrawal of American soldiers. Stabilizing the country and preparing the Afghan army to assume power should be the priority, because it would allow the Afghan people to govern themselves and more attention can be given to eradicating the threat of al Qaeda. It would also give our economy a much-needed economic boost. It was reported by CNN that Defense Secretary Robert Gates stated the insurgents in Afghanistan will continue fighting for as long as there is the presence of foreign forces, as past wars have proven. His insight is on point, and even more so, if the peace offer is rejected and coalition forces remain in combat, militants from all across the region who resent America will pick up arms. That would undoubtedly put a strain on the soldiers, particularly those who have been deployed for a substantial period of time and for those who have been redeployed. Our soldiers are fighting under duress, and the perils of war have caused an alarming number of soldiers to commit suicide. Our government must develop an exit strategy to end the war without compromising its reasons for invading in the first place. Although thousands of al Qaeda and Taliban militants have been killed, and many still die daily, the fighting will continue, and attacks on American and NATO soldiers will only become more deadly. Essentially, because religious wars (commonly called holy wars) versus conventional wars are fought on two different levels. In this instance, freedom fighters or militants fight in the name of Allah or God, seek divine help in combating the enemy. They pray, fast, and die on the battlefield while visualizing victory. Their goal is either victory or martyrdom. Accepting defeat is never an option, even when the invaders are ten times their number and more advanced in military technology. In contrast, conventional wars seek to establish control, maintain power, and force the combatant into surrender. The invaders are given an order by their commander to fight; this justifies their reason for combat. They will continue their aggression until they either become victorious or it becomes evident their objective cannot be met. The war in

Afghanistan is far from over, and too many lives have been lost. President Obama made history, and he entered it shouldering a huge responsibility not only on the domestic front but on the global front as well. America has been on a destructive path for the past several years; this is made evident by our current state of the union. Nevertheless, our nation is a strong nation, and it has the human resources and vision to lead the world to the path of peace. We must believe that it can be done, and if peace is what we desire, each of us has a moral responsibility to make a contribution. Although it may be unpopular by some, protesting the war is not an unpatriotic act; rather, it is a patriotic expression taken by thousands of conscientious people worldwide who believe the invasion was unjustified. Similarly, thousands have supported the war and believe our nation is more secure with our soldiers fighting and stationed abroad. However, the members of the Taliban regard themselves as guardians of the faith who must defend and preserve their land and religion. They believe the fight for Afghanistan and Iraq is a religious jihad that obligates them to engage the enemy with any and all resources. It would be a false assumption and a misguided belief to think they would ever surrender or discontinue their struggle to remove the occupiers from their land. Although the coalition forces have high-tech, sophisticated military equipment, that does not mean they will win the war. Fighting on foreign soil is always a disadvantage to the invader, and it make it that much more difficult to win. At this point, the combined death toll of American and NATO soldiers is approximately 5,600, which is significantly lower than the militants. This serves as an example of the reality of combat, even when the allied weapons are more precise and deadly. Without any question, terrorism is a global threat, and depending on the direction of the two wars, America can become a major target and the center place of violence in the West, similar to that of Israel in the East. President Obama must follow his wisdom. He must seek the advice of his cabinet, but he must keep his faith in the Creator, and pray for a way to bring the wars to an end.

With the U.S. soldiers in combat on several fronts around the world, it is easy to imagine that the violent acts of terrorism will soon find targets on our soil. Unfortunately, just as the extremist and fanatics dress themselves in body explosives to kill innocent men, women, and children in places such as Israel, Iraq, and Pakistan, this sort of violence will soon be seen in places such as New York, Chicago, and Washington. Our intelligence agencies work diligently to locate and keep known individuals with ties or suspected ties to radical organizations under surveillance, but most of these individuals will not be known until a horrific act of violence occurs, leaving body parts of the innocent scattered in our streets and marketplace. The senseless acts of violence such as described occur daily in many countries around the world, and it would be beyond the imagination of most Americans to entertain the idea that it could happen on our soil, but it can. Terrorism is a persistent threat to our nation, and we must remain vigilant on all levels to protect our security. Terrorism is devastating not only because it prematurely takes the life of innocent people, but also because the face of the terrorist has no face. He or she wears many disguises, and their lifestyle could be that of a peasant or an executive in corporate America. In other words, they could be a neighbor, a co-worker, or even a relative—and not be known by anyone. What makes them different from the average American citizen is not their race, ethnicity, or legal status; rather, it is their religious devotion and their willingness to make the ultimate sacrifice (or their willingness to die for a secular cause) that sets them apart. Undoubtedly, the wave of terrorism has escalated and its devastation has reached the four corners of the Earth. America has become a vulnerable nation, and is no longer the safe haven it used to be. Our government must utilize all resources to protect its citizens, and prevent the occurrence of another 9/11 attack. In that regard, all existing hate organizations of any ethnicity must not be tolerated. They must be identified, thoroughly investigated, uprooted, and dismantled. Similarly, any potential hate organization must be targeted and dissolved in its incubation stage. Although most terrorist organizations have long-term objectives, they essentially live from day to day. They are well aware that their activities have deadly consequences, and the possibility of death or imprisonment for life is a daily reality. Therefore, obtaining wealth for personal gain and pursuing influential positions in the secular world is secondary to their ultimate goal. Destruction is their mindset; this is definitely a serious threat, but the idea is normal to them and to those who share their twisted philosophy. Fighting terrorism of this magnitude is obviously life-threatening, serious business that must be dealt with immediately. However, the suspects can be invisible to most of us, and they can even be off the intelligence radar and quite elusive for years. I don't think anyone would argue that all threats involving our national security must be taken seriously, whether the threat is from a known organization that publicly express hate and condemnation, or from an unknown organization. America has entered into a new era in this twenty-first century, and we must face the reality that we are at war with some of the most deadly minds of our time. There are no rules and no borders, and their objective is to shake the foundation of this great nation; our goal is to prevent that from happening. The American spirit is strong, but it must be rejuvenated by unifying the country as one strong nation.

The *Madrassas* of America

The Federal Bureau of Prisons and the State Department of Corrections are the *madrassas* of America. They are the breeding grounds for potential terrorist. A *madrassa* is an Arabic word which means a school, center, or institution for learning. In Islamic countries, students attend a *madrassa* to be educated in math, sciences, and literature—similar to students in America attending public or private school. However, the major difference between the two is that there is no separation of church and state, and the study of the Holy Qur'an is the foundation of the curriculum. Islam is reported to be one of the fastest-growing religions not only in the penal system but in America. The religion of Islam has five fundamental principles that all Muslims must believe and adhere to. They are as follows: To believe that there is only one deity, Allah, and that Muhammad

Ibn Abdullah is His messenger and last prophet; to pray five times a day facing Mecca; to pay a percentage of your annually income to charity; to fast during the Holy Month of Ramadan; and to make the pilgrimage to Mecca at least once. Islam also have many *madhhabs* (pronounced mat-thabs) or schools of thought, and *figh* (religious jurisprudence) which governs the practice, thinking, and sets the perimeter for legislation. However, there are four major *madhhabs* that dominate the thinking and practice of about three-quarters of Muslims throughout the world. They are the schools of Hanafi, Maliki, Shafi'i and Hanbali. All were *imams* (spiritual leaders) in the early stages of Islam after the death of the Prophet Muhammad Ibn Abdullah (may the peace and blessings of Allah be upon Him). Each *imam* had hundreds of thousands of followers as well as scholars that accepted their methodology of interpretations regarding the *hadiths* (the legacy, practice, and teachings of the Prophet Muhammad (pbuh). They were devout Muslims known for their knowledge and nobility. The four *madhhabs* are universally accepted by Muslims all over the world, but only one school of thought is usually taught and practiced by a specific community. However, the ideology can become quite complicated when different practices are incorporated from the different schools of thought. Nevertheless, it is the overall practice of the religion that defines the *madhhad,* which ultimately determines how an individual understands the precepts of the religion. In other words, *extremist* and *fanatic* are terms used to describe an individual that practices the religion at either extreme. However, the true practice of Islam is balanced and it is more moderate than extreme. In the Federal Bureau of Prisons, for example, there is a large population of international prisoners who resent the American government. Many are confined for committing some of the most sophisticated—as well as notorious—crimes. Many have attended some of the finest universities in the world, and they are educated and schooled in the different schools of thought. For the most part, prisoners seeking redemption and change are often attracted to the fundamental principles of a religion, in this case, Islam. At some point during their incarceration, they have done some soul searching and have introspectively decided to make a change. Feelings of remorse, regret, and self-pity undoubtedly contribute to their change of heart, and some are more serious about change than others. In that regard, a prisoner will be influenced by either a gang or a religion. The religious conversion is always much easier because it is acceptable to prison officials, and it minimizes the level of threat in the institution. Conversely, gang association is always viewed in a negative light, because it is usually a violent group of individuals who demand respect and seek to establish control within the institution. It is a well-documented fact by the Federal Bureau of Prisons and the Department of Justice that there are numerous gangs in the penal system. It is also a little-known fact that shortly after entering the system, every prisoner must make a choice regarding gang affiliation before being released into the general prison population. There is no middle ground or room for indecisiveness. A prisoner will either be affiliated with a gang or religion, or will run the risk of being prey. However, gang affiliation seldom requires the initiation that gangs in free society often mandate. When incarcerated, what is usually required is a verbal commitment of brotherhood and a display of solidarity. Behind the wall, gangs usually have designated areas in the dining hall, gym, and recreation area within the cell block. These areas are not approved by the officials as designated areas for any particular group; however, for the safe operations of the institution, prison officials remain vigilant of other non-gang members' activities in the area. These respective areas are designated by the gang leader and known to all other prisoners. Violating an unofficial rule by a non-gang member can be a real problem. The lack of respect can cause a serious disruption within the institution, which can often lead to fights, stabbings, killings, and sometimes a riot. Throughout the prison system, Muslims are known to be organized, they have earned their respect, and they conduct themselves in a peaceful yet fearless matter. They seek to establish a certain level of social balance within the prison to allow the organization to worship, practice, and teach their religion without any problem. They are known to socialize among themselves, and reject any attempts by outsiders to interfere in their activities. Nonetheless, conflict usually occurs when a gang member disrespects someone or seeks to take advantage of a practicing Muslim. If the problem or situation is not mutually resolved, the consequences can be deadly for both prisoner and guard. Statistics have shown that the majority of prisoners are affiliated with some type of gang within the prison system, and they are responsible for most of the violence that occurs. As previously mentioned, there is no middle ground, and everyone knows their association. Also, while living behind the wall, an inactive gang member is equal to a dead gang member. He or she would be ostracized and an open target. Furthermore, there is no such thing as an inactive gang member in the general population. Any inactive members must be removed from the prison population and placed in segregation for their own protection. Prison life is a difficult experience and every day presents a new challenge to survive. In some cases, problems within the prison can be a problem or an opportunity for some members on the outside. There have been documented cases of extortion and even murder of rival gang members orchestrated by the imprisoned leader. Members of the respective groups/gangs are known to have reliable networks of communication that transcend the prison walls. Resources are shared and contacts are made to keep the organization functional both within and without the institution. Also, it is a known fact that international prisoners' philosophy and their perspective on Islam can influence the thinking of a great number of American Muslims, especially new converts. Depending on the orientation, the teachings can be presented in such a way to lay the foundation for either a radical view or a moderate thinker. Nonetheless, converting to Islam while incarcerated can be a benefit as well as a disadvantage. A major benefit is that it will allow an individual to recognize a power greater than oneself. It encourages self-improvement and develops a sense of belonging with others seeking peace of mind in an unnatural prison environment. On the other hand, the disadvantage comes as a result of being stereotyped by prison officials as being defiant, radical, and anti-establishment or anti-America. This can result in such a person being treated differently from the general population or being viewed as just another gang member hiding behind a religion. Admittedly, some of the stereotypes may be true for those who are not serious about the religion. It can also be true for those that have accepted a twisted *mahhab* as their school of thought, and embraced the religion from a radical perspective. The twisted concepts are usually taught by foreign Muslims who have animosity toward America and have not accepted the reality of their situation of being confined for committing a crime. Rather, they are disgruntled toward the criminal justice system, and blame everyone else for their situation instead of accepting responsibility. However, the practice of the majority who embrace the religion and the philosophy of mainstream Islam are quite different. Their practice is what attracts others to the religion. In free society, it is perhaps the philosophy, personal encounters, and social interactions with Muslims who others find comfort and a desire to change. Islam is a universal, complete way of life. It is a monotheistic religion that promotes peace, unity, and love for humanity. If the penal system is ever reformed, it will be the result of the influence of Islam that will effect a positive transformation throughout the system. Islam is growing rapidly in America, and the numbers are registered for both new converts and foreign born Muslims living the in U.S. A spokesperson for the Department of Homeland Security recently stated that approximately 7,000 immigrants displaced by the war since the Iraqi invasion have been allowed into the country. It is also projected that an additional 5,000 will be admitted by the end of 2009. These numbers are small in comparison to the amounts that have been accepted by other countries. However, the numbers contribute to the growth of Islam in this country, and it should highlight the need to understand the religion and what it represents. America is going through a transformation period, and the face of the nation has changed. The American government, as well as its citizens, must necessarily change their view of Islam and their perspective of the Muslim population. In spite of the horrific acts that devastated our nation on September 11, 2001, Islam is a religion of peace that promotes unity and brotherhood. Although America is a country that respects free speech and religion, it has never embraced the religion of Islam as it has accepted other non-Christian faiths. Now that our foreign policy has become a little more flexible as it relates to accepting immigrants from Islamic countries, attention must now be given to a religion that has made numerous contributions to ancient and modern civilization. The growth of Islam in America is not a plan orchestrated by man; rather, it is a divine plan of the Creator, to bless America with the peace and tranquility that the religion brings. In the penal systems of American, when there is a religious conversion for African-Americans, an overwhelming number have gravitated to the religion of Islam. The reason for this conversion is two-fold. The first is because African Americans represent a large number of the prison population, and they view it as a religion of defiance and self-containment. Meaning Islam teaches an individual to be spiritually strong, confident, and submit to no man or system; submission is only to the Creator. Therefore, for the most part, the majority of prisoners have some kind of resentment toward the criminal justice system either because of personal experience or its perceived injustice, and that belief is reflected in their behavior. Practicing the religion of Islam while confined is a form of freedom in that it encourages an individual to focus on the concept of *jihad* (the internal struggle to improve oneself) and acknowledge the Creator of the universe. That concept and acknowledgment is the driving force that keeps the mind free, and motivates an individual to seek his or her freedom. Recently, five foreign-born Muslims were convicted in the United States District Court of New Jersey for conspiracy to kill American soldiers stationed at the Fort Dix army base. All five were living in the country legally, and three were employed. None of the five were connected to al Qaeda or any other extremist organization, and all five pled not guilty to the charges brought against them by the United States Attorney's Office. However, the FBI had infiltrated their social organization with an informant who wore a body wire to record conversations regarding their plot. During the course of the trial, three of the defendants had stated during cross-examination that they had resentment toward the U.S. government for invading Afghanistan and Iraq. They alleged the American government had declared war on Islam, and was systematically killing Muslims for no reason. Although they admitted to making several statements expressing condemnation of America, they denied the charge of plotting to kill American soldiers. Prior to this incident, a similar incident involving Muslims allegedly plotting to bomb an international airport occurred in New York. A total of six people were arrested and charged with conspiracy to attack and/or bomb a government institution. All were tried in the

United States District Court of New York and four were convicted. During the course of the trial, the United States prosecutor was unable to link the men to an extremist organization. However, it was established that the two foreign-born Muslims had attended a mosque in their native land of Pakistan that the U.S. government suspected of having ties to a radical organization that was in opposition to the Pakistani government. The other two who were convicted were African Americans who had served time in state institutions, and were disgruntled toward the government for discriminating against African Americans and Muslims. A similar incident involving Muslims in Texas occurred when they were arrested through the joint efforts of the FBI and DEA for trying to purchase weapons from an undercover agent. Those arrested contended they were entrapped by the government, because the idea to obtain weapons was initiated by an undercover agent working for the federal government. These are just a few examples of Muslims being arrested and convicted of crimes that had the potential to become deadly if government officials were not proactive in their investigations. Although these individuals were arrested and subsequently convicted and incarcerated, all were connected to either an organization or movement that they believed they were targeted because of their religious beliefs. Incidents such as these and many others with similar characteristics throughout the nation show how an individual can become disgruntled and develop negative sentiments toward the government. As more attacks against Muslims occur throughout America, more incidents of criminal behavior and activity will become more evident. Particularly, our criminal justice system began targeting Muslim women for wearing the *hijab* (head scarf)—while overlooking the head scarf of other religions that also mandate covering the head. That is an act of religious discrimination that feeds the radical mind. Reiterating a point previously made, Islam is a religion of peace, but when the women of any religion in a civilized society are being persecuted and disrespected by the legislative branch of our government, that is equivalent to being stripped of their dignity. Consequently, without advocating violence in any respect, the men must rise to their defense and protect them at all cost and by any legal means necessary. Islam is rooted in this country, and we as a nation must become more educated, tolerant, and understanding. In regard to Guantanamo Bay, I think it would be a good political move as well as advancement in humanity if the United States government closed the torture facility as President Obama has mandated. Many officials in Washington support this decision. Closing the military prison would help restore America's image in the international community, and it would save our government millions of dollars. Additionally, closing the prison can be the first step toward restoring diplomatic ties with Cuba after a forty-seven-year trade embargo. At some point, the prison can be open as a public attraction that would detail the painful history of the facility as it relates to the infamous 9/11 attack. The idea is similar to that of Alcatraz in the San Francisco Bay and Robbins Island in South Africa, both of which recount a turbulent time in history. It can become a major tourist attraction for people all over the world, generating substantial revenues that could create employment opportunities for both Cubans and Americans. Although I think closing the facility is an excellent idea, one of the major problems with closing the Cuban facility is where to relocate the prisoners. Most of the prisoners have not been afforded the opportunity to consult with an attorney, some have not been charged with any offense, and others have been charged with some of the most serious offenses against our government. Generally speaking, all have been classified as being dangerous or high-profile prisoners and terrorists, and that requires special classification. Transfers to federal penitentiaries within the Federal Bureau of Prisons seems to be the only option at this point. Although there are numerous federal penitentiaries throughout America, there are not enough military penitentiaries to house the more than 200 prisoners involved. Therefore, the options are limited to either deporting them to their native country, deporting them to a neighboring country that is willing to accept them, scatter those convicted throughout the prisons in mainland America, or allow those with relatives living in the U.S. to remain. In any event, having convicted terrorists confined within the states could present a serious threat to our national security, and could possibly accelerate terrorist activities within the mainland. Although these prisoner will be monitored 24/7, and will have minimum contact with the outside world. Unless they have a special classification under The Terrorist Act and are thereby segregated from the general population, they will be afforded the same privileges as all other prisoners. Accordingly, they must be in the general prison population, they must be afforded visiting privileges, and they must be permitted to worship and practice their religion just as all the other prisoners can. In many countries around the world, some of these men are highly respected and have an unknown number of followers. They are seen by many as potential martyrs because they are combatant soldiers/militants/terrorists who have fought to defend and preserve Islam, and were captured during the jihad. In our criminal justice system, many of these prisoners will be convicted and will probably be in prison for a long time, perhaps for life. In that regard, the reality is that they will possibly die in prison, and get the reward of paradise. With that possibility in mind, as their trials proceed through our criminal justice system, Muslims who study their ideology will internalize their feelings, divorce themselves from the secular world, and seek to die as martyrs themselves. It will only take one act of self-sacrifice on America's soil before similar acts will follow. As history has proven time and again, when an individual decides to make the ultimate sacrifice, there is nothing or no one that can prevent them from carrying out the act. Accordingly, the decision to deport international prisoners to their homeland must be open to serious discussion, and the advantages as well as the disadvantages must be seriously considered. It was reported by CNN that some of the prisoners who were deported to their homeland have returned to the battlefield. That practice will continue as long as their country is at war. Unfortunately, no action or decision concerning the fate of those in custody can be made until the Pentagon makes a decision regarding the direction of the war. Until then, the American people can never really be safe, and there is little our government can do to insure otherwise. Fortunately, there has not been a terrorist attack on American soil since the infamous 9/11 attack that can be contributed to either al Qaeda or any other international radical organization. Our Department of Homeland Security must remain vigilant of our borders, and must continue to share intelligence information with our intelligence community to allow us to stay one step ahead of terror.

The Search for
Osama bin Laden

CNN recently released a twenty-two-minute audio/ video of Osama bin Laden condemning the Israeli massacre of the Palestinians, and calling for an *intifada* against the Jewish state. A similar call was also made by Khaled Meshal, the supreme leader of Hamas, when the conflict first began. The video undoubtedly removed any question as to whether Osama was dead or alive. Some in the intelligence community had speculated that he was killed when the U.S. repeatedly bombed the mountains of Tora Bora in response to intercepted intelligence information stating he was spotted in the area. However, the question has now been answered. Osama bin Laden is still alive, and looking quite healthy after living in the mountains for so many years. He is still the undisputed leader of al Qaeda, and he is the mastermind who keeps the organization operational. Unlike his partner, Ayman al-Zawahiri, who has released more than nine video messages in the past twelve months condemning America, Osama seldom appears on video, but when he does, his message always bring a chill of terror to the minds of most Americans because of the 9/11 attack. As expected, he has strategically retreated from the front line of command only to lead the organization from the rear. His call for *jihad* to Muslims to fight against the Israeli aggression is going to bring a new wave of terror to the Middle East. His influence spans the four corners of the Earth, and his declarations seem to always reach the ears of the radical mind. Osama has been hunted by the U.S. for eight years, but his capture still remains beyond our reach. Quite frankly, I don't think he will be captured alive as Saddam Hussein was. I believe he has a huge ego, and his extreme views on Islam would not allow him to be extradited to the United States—a country that is certain to humiliate him, give him more than fifteen minutes of fame, and broadcast his picture around the world. After that, he would be tried, convicted, and swiftly executed. Rather, I think he would die in the midst of combat as a martyr, and any member of his immediate circle would be there to defend him until death, while killing as many American and NATO soldiers as possible before becoming martyrs themselves. Osama bin Laden's recent message leads me to believe that he will attempt another attack on America (probably within the first year of Obama's presidency) to prove that he is still in charge, in spite of the fact that the recent conflict in the Middle East between Israel and the Palestinians have ended. Also, because he is aware that there will be a substantial increase in American soldiers in the region within months, which will increase his chances of being captured. In spite of the change in administration in Washington, the objectives are still the same as it relates to capturing Osama and destroying al Qaeda. The aftermath of 9/11 has left the American people psychologically traumatized; the memory of that infamous day is embedded in our minds. The reality is that it could happen again. President Obama has stated that he is going to intensify the search to capture bin Laden, and if Osama no longer has the support and protection of the Taliban (as is speculated by our intelligence agencies), Osama bin Laden will probably be located and killed within the first two years of the new administration. I suspect that if this information is true, his location and death will probably happen as a result of intercepted intelligence information from a high-ranking Taliban commander who was once loyal to him. This person will unwittingly disclose his location to a field operative without regard for his continued safety. The $25 million reward that has been offered by the U.S. as a reward for information leading to his capture has proven not to be an incentive, primarily because providing information of his location to the invader would be tantamount to be branded a traitor, with the punishment being death. Also, but not as important, the informer would not live long enough to enjoy spending the money, even in exile. Ayman al-Zawahiri, the second in command of al Qaeda, is seeking martyrdom by his repeated exposure to the Internet. He seems to enjoy posting derogatory and condemning messages toward America and President Obama. The various messages have been authenticated by CIA Director Michael Hayden, and they confirm that he is also alive and well. The threatening remarks he has made against "the criminals in America" is a clear testament of his intentions to plot, plan, and hopefully execute further attacks against America. President Obama has stated that his strategy to capture both Osama and Ayman al-Zawahiri is to withdraw a substantial amount of troops from Iraq, and increase the numbers in Afghanistan. General Petraeus, however, believes both terrorists are hiding in caves somewhere in the mountains that border Pakistan and Afghanistan. Therefore, the increase of troops will provide additional support to the coalition forces, as well as the Afghan government during its complete transition to power. Assuming that Mullah Omar, the Taliban leader, decides to renounce violence and participate in the government—as suggested by President Hamib Karzai—the transition to power would occur with minimal resistance. However, there has been no indication that he will accept. Meanwhile, our soldiers will unfortunately continue to die defending the Afghan government, and our nation will always be under the threat of being attacked as long as Osama bin Laden is at large. Without a doubt, al Qaeda's infrastructure must be dismantled and its leaders must be captured. Otherwise, the war in Afghanistan will be ongoing and the body count will continue to rise. There is no other solution to this problem. Nevertheless, equally as important is the need to educate the American people about the true meaning and teachings of Islam. Islam is a religion that promotes human excellence, and it moves the whole of humanity forward because of its submission to the Creator. There is no compulsion in the religion, and it certainly forbids the killing of innocent people, particularly the killing of women and children under any circumstance. The people who commit those acts against mankind are backward in their practice of religion, and they have a total disregard for human life.

President Obama has stated that he intends to address the Muslim world from a Muslim country within the first 100 days of his administration. The purpose of the visit and address is to inform the Muslim world that America is not its enemy, and that the opportunity to establish a conciliatory dialogue to bridge the gap of political and culture misunderstandings should be discussed. Also, his visit is to seek the support of the Arab world in the global fight against terrorism, especially al Qaeda, which not only threatens America, it threatens the world. In light of the fact that the events in the Middle East and the Muslim world are so volatile, President Obama's visit would make a huge impact on in the political arena. This will allow him to be in a better position to broker peace in the region. The world has applauded his election as the new commander in chief, and Muslims throughout the world have perceived him as the catalyst for change.

THE HISTORIC INAUGURATION 2009

The inauguration of President Barack Hussein Obama as the forty-fourth president of the United States of America was a phenomenal event. A modest estimate is that approximately 2 million people from all across the nation attended this historical event. As I looked into the crowd, I saw the "dream" that Dr. Martin Luther King envisioned more than forty-five years ago when he delivered his famous "I Have a Dream" speech on the National Mall in the nation's capital. There was a sea of people of all hues—black, white, brown, and yellow—from the United States Capitol to the Washington Monument and beyond. People of all races, ethnicities, religions, and genders braved the bitter cold to witness the swearing-in of the first African-American president in American history. The display of unity was so astounding that it dispelled any doubt that America is indeed the great nation it prides itself to be. History is unfolding right before our eyes, and we must continue to move the country forward. We must not allow the accomplishments of the past to be lost to the future because of our narrow vision. President Obama represents change, and his vision is to unite all Americans as one union, under the leadership of one American president. The racism and racial divide that has kept this country divided for far too long must be eradicated. We must envision hope and challenge ourselves to do better. We are confronted with many issues in this twenty-first century—particularly racism—and we must change our perceptions and our ways of thinking about each other to overcome the racist mindset that hinders us from making substantial human and racial progress. America has always been a nation that leads, and we have made outstanding accomplishments in science, medicine, and technology. However, the racism that plagues the mind of so many Americans has caused us as a nation to fall short in advancing humanity. Therefore, as we witnessed this milestone in history with pride and jubilation, my heart bleeds because of the massacre of the Palestinian people. The world witnessed the killing of 1,300 men, women, and children in a matter of three weeks by the Israeli government, and little was said or done. More than 2,200 homes were completely destroyed, leaving innocent victims without shelter. As previously mentioned, our government, under the Bush administration, stood by while those horrific acts were taking place and did absolutely nothing to intervene. Hypothetically thinking, imagine America being under siege; the chosen battleground for terrorism is any small city in the country. Although we have unfortunately experienced targeted disasters on our soil by disgruntled citizens and foreign terrorists, we have not experienced daily war activity and particularly not air attacks. That idea is beyond the imagination of any sane-minded individual, and we must prevent that horrible nightmare from ever becoming a reality on our soil. Although this was a great day for most Americans, we must not forget the events of the past, especially the wars initiated by our government. President Obama is the new commander in chief, and he must chart a new course for our nation. He must regain the respect of the international community by departing from the Bush philosophy of arrogant democracy, and establish himself as the leader and visionary he truly is. He has the integrity and the leadership ability to not only change America, but his positive image and his willingness to extend the hand of peace can also change the world. He should not be criticized in a degrading way by any American citizen, especially to get attention in the political arena. Since being sworn in as president, his administration has contributed approximately $118 million toward the reconstruction of the Gaza Strip as well as for humanitarian aid. The contribution is a positive gesture that will change the lives of so many disenfranchised people, and several countries have followed our lead. People around the globe, from the small villages in Kenya to the penthouse in Washington, have celebrated his election, and the opportunity to broker peace must not be delayed another day. I believe the Lord of all the Worlds has blessed America, and President Barack Hussein Obama has been chosen to fulfill a divine mission. We must support him. Let us pray the prayer of peace, the *Al Fatiha*.

In the Name of God, the Most Gracious, the Most Merciful, Praise be to God the Cherisher and Sustainer of the worlds, Most Gracious, Most Merciful, Master of the Day of Judgment. Thee do we worship and Thine aid we seek. Show us the Straight Way, the way of those on whom Thou hast bestowed Thy grace, those whose portion is not wrath, and who go not astray.

The Holy Qur'an, the Opening

ABOUT THE AUTHOR

The author is an African-American citizen born in the United States. He converted to the religion of Islam in 1978 prior to the Iranian Revolution. He has studied under some of the most knowledgeable Muslims in the Islamic world, where he gained a comprehensive understanding of their culture, beliefs, and their perception of America as it relates to its view of Islam. He is a practicing Muslim, and he is currently working for one of the most prestigious institutions in America.

www.ingramcontent.com/pod-product-compliance
Lightning Source LLC
Chambersburg PA
CBHW021242280526
45784CB00005B/2199